Celestial Enchantment

Celestial Enchantment

Matthew Edward Petchinsky

Celestial Enchantment: The Mystic Tree of Dreams